Mastering the Public Cloud

A practical guide to a winning cloud strategy, workload migration, cloud management and optimisation.

Oliver Surdival

Published on Kindle Direct Publishing

Publication Date: March 2020

Author photograph by Martin Kuzmicz

Sold by: Amazon

ISBN - 9798630593238

For Lorraine, Arron, Shannon and Dylan

"Our industry does not respect tradition. It only respects innovation."

Satya Nadella

Thank you

To my family, for enduring and supporting me over the
last several months.

To Niamh Doyle, my beautiful sister-in-law, for your
support and thorough review, thank you.

About the Author

Oliver Surdival

Oliver Surdival is a business & technology leader who is passionate about cloud and in particular the public cloud. Oliver started his first technology company developing software back in 2005, which was acquired five years later. Oliver has over a decade of experience running and operating his own public cloud service business which was successfully acquired in 2018 by Irelands largest managed service provider, Arkphire ltd.

Over the past ten years, Oliver and his team have helped hundreds of organisations successfully migrate workloads to the public cloud with a winning cloud strategy. Oliver sits on various boards, advising and helping organisations to achieve their profitability and growth ambitions enabled by the public cloud.

Oliver lives in the west of Ireland and is married with three beautiful children. He is passionate about creating jobs and opportunities in the west of Ireland and has invested in many start-ups, giving his time for free to help and advise businesses in the west to expand.

Content

Introduction

Your board of directors have just made the decision that the business needs to be more innovative and agile to keep pace with its competitors. You have been asked to develop your organisation migration strategy and move all the workloads to the cloud to take advantage of the public cloud capabilities.

When meeting with CIOs and senior business leaders, It's funny how often the above happens, leaving you with the responsibility to transition your organisation IT infrastructure to the cloud, initially with unrealistic budgets and timeframes. I'm often told that moving to the cloud is a high priority within organisations. Almost without fail the next question is "How do we get started.", "What workloads can we migrate.", "Can you help us develop our cloud and migration strategy. ", and "How will the migration to the cloud change the way the organisation operates.". All the above questions are very valid, and my team and I have helped hundreds of organisations develop and implement their migration to the cloud.

The goal of this book is to give the reader the knowledge and insights from real-world experience and the ability to develop their organisation's own migrations strategy and techniques to implement the migration plan. You will learn the different cloud terms, concepts, models and strategies to develop a winning cloud strategy for your organisation. What workloads you should move first and how to migrate those workloads to the cloud.

Back in 2010, I first heard the word cloud as a platform to deliver IT infrastructure and services which piqued my interest considerably; all the signs indicating it would become the Next Big Thing. I immediately started to investigate the cloud opportunity to see if there was a market trend; I could take advantage of. Having a background in IT and software development, I was quite comfortable to invest in my startup business that would focus on delivering cloud solutions. Just before I set up my cloud business, I got a lucky break when an existing client asked if we did cloud to which I quickly replied: "Of course, what are you looking for?" My seminal client needed email and a web-based collaborative platform, which we delivered. That was in 2011, I sold my software development business to fund my new startup, and that's how I started my journey to the cloud.

I sincerely hope that after reading and reflecting on each chapter within this book that you will have gained the knowledge and insights to develop your own winning cloud strategy.

Oliver Surdival
April 2020

- CHAPTER 1 -

Public Cloud History

A brief history of the cloud

"The cloud services companies of all sizes...The cloud is for everyone. The cloud is a democracy." ~ Marc Benioff, Founder, CEO and Chairman of Salesforce.

Cloud computing has completely revolutionised the way organisations operate and consumes IT resources. The adoption of the public cloud has been on a steep rise as more and more organisations recognise its benefits for their long-term IT plans. The cloud-related spending is expected to grow at a rate that is six times more than that of general IT spending through the year 2020; Cloud computing technology was driven by an essential business requirement, return on investment. Since the 1950s, businesses used mainframe computers which were extremely expensive to purchase.

To maximise the return on investment on the mainframe equipment, the organisation would purchase multiple desktop computers and implement a time-sharing schedule to allow employees access and connect to the mainframe; this is the foundation of cloud computing.

In the 1960s a computer scientist called J.C.R. Licklider had the idea for interconnected systems of computers. In 1969 Bob Taylor and Larry Roberts built on Licklider idea developing ARPANET (Advanced Research Projects Agency Network).

ARPANET is commonly recognised as the first network that allowed data to be shared between computers that were in different geographical locations. You may understand this type of technology where you can remotely access your data; we know this as cloud computing.

AWS – THE HOW AND WHY

AWS is the world's first hyper-scale public cloud provider and is the pioneers of modern public cloud technology. AWS launched their first service Elastic Compute back in August of 2006 and have grown to be the largest hyper-scale public cloud provider worth an estimated half a trillion dollars.

Back in the 2000s, Amazon was an e-commerce business, and they had a requirement to launch a new service called Merchant.com that would allow third-party businesses to build an online store on top of their hugely successful e-commerce platform. To build a third-party platform that could scale with various services proved to be very difficult.

The amazon business was growing fast and recruiting new developers to support growth. However, with the addition of extra developers, they were not building or deploying new applications any quicker. When the amazon team investigated further, they found that a typical project would take three months to complete, much of that time consumed by installing the hardware, configuring the storage, backups and building the database.

Each development team worked in silos, building their system per project with little to no thought of reusing expensive infrastructure for other projects. To solve this problem, the team at amazon built a common infrastructure service layer that all the engineers could access, increasing application build time, increasing agility and reducing costs. The Amazon development team could deploy resources from a massive pool of shared infrastructure, which the development team was not responsible for managing. That's when amazon realised; they had something that could revolutionise the IT landscape. Through solving their internal problem, the team at amazon had developed core capabilities at running and managing reliable, scalable, cost-effective infrastructure.

AWS works as a considerable Infrastructure-as-a-Service (IaaS); it serves as a medium that is used to solve most of the cloud-related issues. AWS provides many complex solutions to cloud-related matters. This is mainly because they give unique services; hence you can gain from its wealth of expertise. They provide a high premium to their services and emphasise more on their performance and excellence.

AWS was first-to-market and had a huge competitive advantage, developed from their years of experience and innovation. It took many years before any competitor reacted to the market opportunity that amazon created. From this innovation, Amazon has a significant market share compared to all the other public cloud providers.

MICROSOFT AZURE

Microsoft was slow to recognise the market opportunity pioneer by AWS. They lost many years of innovation and market share that they may never clawback. Microsoft was never known to be the most innovative company, but as a software giant trying to make inroads into obvious opportunities like smartphone and gaming. Microsoft announced in 2008 that they would be entering the public cloud market and on the First of February 2010, Microsoft Azure (Formally Windows Azure) was released.

Stand back and hold your breath, Satya Nadella was announced as the new CEO of Microsoft on 4 February 2014. Nadella got straight to work by modernising Microsoft mission statement to "empower every person and every organisation on the planet to achieve more". Nadella promoted two critical concepts for the modern business of 'mobile-first, cloud-first' and created several new services around this, guiding Microsoft to integrate all its solutions.

"We live in a mobile-first and cloud-first world. Computing is ubiquitous and experiences span devices and exhibit ambient intelligence. Billions of sensors, screens and devices in conference rooms, living rooms, cities, cars, phones, PCs are forming a vast network and streams of data that simply disappear into the background of our lives," said Nadella.

Nadella has overseen Microsoft acquisition strategy with its vast cash reserves to acquire companies of all sizes. They purchased LinkedIn in 2016 for $26 billion, Github in 2018 for $7.5 billion alongside several smaller businesses to fill gaps in security, development, productivity and cloud services.

Microsoft is the second-largest public cloud provider behind AWS, but this may change in the future due to recent landmark wins such as the $10 billion cloud contract with the Pentagon. Many experts say this win puts Azure in the same league as AWS.

GOOGLE CLOUD PLATFORM

Google announced in April 2008 that they were entering the public cloud market with the release of their app engine. The App engine platform had capabilities of hosting and scaling web applications, and this was the first Google public cloud service.

In a strategic move to gain market share, recognition and feedback, Google announced that the app engine service would be free to the first 10,000 customers to run their applications in the cloud. Since its initial launch date in 2008, Google has developed its public cloud service into a premier offering. GCP has grown its public cloud platform services including compute, storage and application development, machine learning and AI.

Google announced in November of 2019, Thomas Kurian to succeed Diane Greene as cloud chief. In one of his first public announcements, he outlined that GCP shall focus on specific industries and work more exclusively with channel partners.

"You will see us accelerate the growth even faster than we have to date,", "We are hiring some of the best talents from around the industry to grow our sales organisation, and you will see us competing much more aggressively as we go forward," said Kurian.
This type of language is a clear indicator that Google is looking to compete and win within the public cloud market.

WHAT IS THE PUBLIC CLOUD?

The public cloud is a pool of virtual resources offered and managed by third-party providers over the public internet. The virtual resources or services are automatically provisioned via a self-service interface and shared between many organisations. A public cloud has several common attributes like

Scalability – allows the organisation to scale resources on-demand to thousands of applications and storage.

Multitenancy – A shared resource model, where multiple users share resources like network, server's hardware, storage and applications.

Elasticity – organisations could increase or decrease resources as required.

Pay as you go – Only pay for resources that you consume.

Self-Provisioning – Users have the ability to provision resources.

The public cloud value proposition has the promise to reduce the total cost of ownership and shift the financial model from fixed to variable cost, CAPEX to OPEX. This change in the financial model enables organisations to free up budgets on capital infrastructure projects, drive innovation and business agility across the organisation.

ADVANTAGES OF THE PUBLIC CLOUD

The public cloud has many advantages in today's world; all organisations need to understand and take advantage of the public cloud capabilities or risk been left behind by their competitors. Below you shall find an overview of some advantages of the public cloud.

Cost-Effectiveness – the shift from Capex to Opex is a considerable advantage to organisations, alongside the flexible pricing structure to pay for resources on demand and turn off expensive services when not in use.

Scalability – Scaling resources on-demand without having the responsibility to manage any of the underlying hardware.

High Reliability – Public cloud is exceptionally reliable with multiple geographical data centre locations, providing hardware and data centre redundancy, making the public cloud services very safe.

Quick and Easy – The larger public cloud providers have over 700 cloud services you can utilise for your business. You can deploy these resources and services in a matter of minutes, making it easy and quick.

Contract terms – Most organisations do not want to sign up to long term contracts, with the cloud; you only pay for what you use and does not require a long-term commitment.

Up to date technology – It is the public cloud vendor responsibility to keep the infrastructure updated to best security, management and compliance practices.

THE CLOUD WAR

Public cloud has been the fastest-growing market for many of the world's largest technology companies. There is an ongoing heavyweight battle between the three public cloud giants. AWS is out in front and remains the clear leaders, followed by Microsoft in second place. Google may be in the last place, but I would not rule them out of the race.

This fierce battle between these giants has driven down cloud prices and accelerated cloud features and services. This has helped many small businesses to grow, allowing them to focus on what they do best instead of managing infrastructure.

AWS v Azure V Google is the ultimate cloud war of all times. This war will go on for several years, and I'm sure there will be surprises along the way.

An important decision that organisations must make in their cloud transformation is which cloud vendor to work with. I would suggest looking at the capabilities for each vendor to solve your business or technology issues and have an open mind to working with all three.

FUTURE OF THE CLOUD

For several years, the IT industry has touted the importance of public cloud computing. Currently, only 41% of workloads run in the public cloud. There is a massive opportunity for the public cloud provider to grow, and this year is just the perfect timing for that.

While lots of companies are trying to use the Cloud for more technical purposes, those kinds of projects are becoming fewer by the day. What we see more often are data centre consolidation and application migration. The present reality is such that brings us to the Cloud 2.0 wave; in this wave, Cloud is not an option; it is a reality, and we are noticing a lot of organisations migrating to this wave of cloud-first and the cloud-only model

- CHAPTER 2 -

Public Cloud 101

Understanding the basics of Public Cloud

"Cloud is about how you do computing, not where you do computing. — Paul Maritz, CEO of VMware.

Public cloud has taken the world by storm, and more and more organisations are using the cloud as an enabler to drive growth and gain market share. It's essential as you start developing your organisation cloud strategy, you have a basic understanding of critical public cloud strategies, terminologies, concepts, technologies, and what the public cloud future will look like.

In this chapter, I'm going to explain a whole range of public cloud strategies and concepts that shall give you a solid foundation in the public cloud space. This foundation shall enable you to make better decisions to develop your organisation's cloud strategy.

CLOUD FIRST STRATEGY

The term 'Cloud-first' has been around for the past decade. In straightforward terms, it means, 'to consider cloud technology before all others. This ought to be when a new IT project crops up, a refresh or replacement is identified.

A cloud-first strategy provides an opportunity for organisations to save costs on infrastructure and increase capabilities. Organisations can subscribe to vendors who offer premium solutions at cheaper rates without setting up their infrastructure stack.

By adopting a cloud-first strategy, organisations can move away from maintaining and managing their on-site technology stack. The rapid growth in the cloud gives even the most limited organisation access to the latest and greatest technology available.

It's becoming more challenging for on-prem alternatives to match the functionality or value of solutions built in the cloud. By subscribing to a cloud provider for software licenses, platform or infrastructure, an organisation can achieve premium services at a regular, guaranteed low cost.

Some of the dangers associated with a cloud-first mindset include identity governance, data security, and compliance. In addition to these, there are less obvious dangers to a cloud-first mindset:

Performance Risk - While companies are getting excited about the opportunity of the cloud, it is worthy to note that the cloud is a layer of different vendors and networks that can influence the performance of applications and user experience.

Misconception about user experience - All clouds are not created equal. For example, the delivery of Salesforce to the end-users differ from that of Microsoft SharePoint. The absence of holistic knowledge about the architectural structure of cloud applications culminates in companies establishing wrong goals of cloud performance.

CLOUD ONLY STRATEGY

A cloud-only strategy is a mandate that compels the organisation to implement cloud-only solutions across the business. In contrast, a cloud-first strategy is a suggestion that the organisation can choose to take or not. A cloud-only strategy can be limiting where alternative solutions are ignored, such as hybrid or on-prem. One of those options may be a better solution and provide more value to the organisation.

PUBLIC CLOUD

The public cloud is based on the standard cloud computing model, in which a service provider makes cloud resources, such as applications and storage, accessible to the general public via the internet. Public cloud services can be free or billed on a pay-per-use basis. It offers organisations an easy and economical set-up and configuration since the costs associated with hardware, applications and networks are borne by the public cloud vendor. Organisations can scale based on requirements; pricing is based on a pay-as-you-use model with a reduction in cost incurred on energy and staff.

PRIVATE CLOUD

A private cloud is a type of cloud that is solely dedicated to one organisation. Private clouds are traditionally operated on-prem; however, there has been a shift from on-prem private cloud to locate the private cloud in a third-party data centre. Private cloud has proprietary architecture and effectively becomes a private cloud when one organisation is dedicated to that hardware with isolated access.

The private cloud has similar benefits as the public like self-service, workforce mobility; provision of workloads; modifications of IT resources on demand; and increased visibility across resource usage. Billing tools monitor the consumption of IT resources and business units pay only for what they use.

At the same time, the hosted service offered by a private cloud is only intended for a limited number of users installed behind a firewall. This approach thus minimises the security risks that some organisations may face in terms of public Cloud. The private cloud also gives the company direct control over its data and security.

An organisation can also combine public and private cloud services as part of the deployment of a hybrid cloud. Thus, if the need of users exceeds the capacities of the private cloud, they have the possibility of calling on the public cloud, a functionality called overload of load (or Cloud bursting).

HYBRID CLOUD

A hybrid cloud is a type of cloud that uses a combination of on-prem, private cloud and public cloud services, with orchestration capacity between the two platforms.

For example, a company could deploy a private cloud on-site to host sensitive or critical workloads but could use a third-party, public cloud provider, such as Google (Compute Engine), to host less-critical resources like testing, validation and development.

A hybrid cloud is particularly valuable in the event of dynamic and highly scalable needs. E.G., a transactional order entry system that experiences peak demand during the holidays season will be the right candidate for the hybrid cloud. The application will run in a private cloud but will use cloud bursting to access additional IT resources in the event of intense activity.

Despite its advantages, the hybrid cloud can present technical and administrative challenges. Private cloud workloads have to access and engage with public cloud providers. As such, a hybrid cloud requires API compatibility and robust network connectivity.

DIFFERENCE BETWEEN PUBLIC, PRIVATE AND HYBRID CLOUD

Vendors like AWS, Microsoft and Google manage and maintain the core infrastructure in a public cloud, whereas the private cloud is managed by your organisation. The initial cost to deploy a public cloud is relatively cheap compared to a private cloud. A hybrid is a mixture of both private and public cloud alongside on-prem.

Public	Hybrid	Private
Services owned and operated by the vendor	Best of both Public and Private clouds	Own the hardware
Maintenance cost paid by the vendor	More deployment options	Higher Security as H/W not shared
Pay as you go model	Increased compliance issues	Increased controls over the environment
Platform is shared	Increased security	Increase compliance
Less control	Can be more expensive to operate	Difficult to scale
Opex expense	Capex & opex expense	Capex expense

MULTI-CLOUD

Multi-cloud is a cloud computing deployment model where businesses use two or more cloud services within their environment. This refers to a mix of SaaS, PaaS and IaaS across different providers like AWS, Azure, GCP, Salesforce, HubSpot etc

"Most organisations adopt a multi-cloud strategy out of a desire to avoid vendor lock-in or to take advantage of best-of-breed solutions," said Michael Warrilow, VP Analyst, Gartner.

CLOUD OPERATING MODEL

What we often see emerging when organisations start adopting the cloud is, they implement the same processes and practices used in a traditional IT environment. The organisation does not optimise their operating model for the cloud, so miss out on the speed, agility and costs savings that the cloud promise.

To maximise the benefits of the cloud, you need to evolve your organisation and the strategies by which you manage your infrastructure applications.

A cloud operating model can be defined as a model or an abstract representation of how an organisation adds value to its client or users via the use of cloud solutions. This is a well-articulated operating model that is tried and tested and has worked overtime.

SHARED RESPONSIBILITY MODEL

Businesses and cloud vendors like AWS, Microsoft and Google are each accountable for specific components of the cloud infrastructure under the shared responsibility model.

It's a well-established framework that outlines precisely what businesses are responsible for like GDPR, HIPAA, NIST and ISO, among others. Customer responsibility will be determined based on the cloud services that the customer chooses. These services will determine the level of configuration that the customer will need to perform as part of their security responsibility.

This model of shared responsibility between the customer and cloud provider also extends to IT controls. Just as responsibility for the execution of the IT environment is shared between the cloud provider and its customers, so is the management, execution and verification of IT controls.

Customer	Responsible for	Customer Data			
	Security in	Platform, Application, Data, Access and Security			
	the cloud	OS, networks, firewalls and database configuration			
		Server-side and network traffic encryption			
Cloud	Responsible for	Compute	Storage	Networks	Database
Vendor	Security of	Regions			
	cloud Infrastructure	Availbility Zones			

The cloud provider can help ease the workload of a customer against runtime controls associated with the physical infrastructure deployed in the cloud environment that may have been previously managed by the customer. As the deployment in the cloud is different for each customer, they can benefit from the transition from the management of specific IT controls to the cloud provider, which creates a (new) distributed control environment.

In a context of shared control, the cloud provides the prerequisites for the infrastructure and, for its part, the customer must ensure the implementation of its own controls as part of its use of cloud services:

· Patch Management: Cloud provider is responsible for correcting infrastructure faults, but the customer is responsible for remedying its operating systems (s) and applications.

· Configuration Management: Cloud provider maintains the configuration of its infrastructure, but the customer must configure its own operating systems, databases and applications.

· Knowledge and training: Cloud provider trains its employees, but the customer is responsible for training their own employees.

SECURITY MODEL

A security strategy enumerates how your business can maintain the security of the cloud environment as well as the data stored there. You need a robust security strategy to guarantee your organisation can work safely and securely in the cloud.

The security model for traditional on-prem to the cloud has fundamentally changed and had flamed the idea that the cloud is not secure. The fundamental shift is from IP-based to using identity-based access. The move to identity-based access is disruptive to traditional security models.

Identity-based security is a method to control access to a digital product or service primarily based on the authenticated identity of an individual. Underpinning the identity-based security approach is the identity-based access controls (IBAC) (or identity-based licensing) concept.

CLOUD OPTIMISATION

The worldwide adoption of public cloud services has fuelled to a degree, the cost concerns that many businesses have. The goal of cloud cost optimisation is to reduce your cloud spend by identifying unused resources, minimise waste, determine the capacity for higher discounts, and re-sizing cloud services to scale.

As cloud computing solutions evolve, applications are being transported to the public cloud. For organisations, it is essential to deliver high-performance at the right cost and security to users. This endeavour will demand to leverage cloud optimisation tools as well as techniques that can enable them to detect and control cost, permitting organisations to select the right course of action.

SERVERLESS

Serverless is a misleading term in one sense, as physical servers are required to run workloads, but the developers are not aware of this infrastructure. Serverless computing is a method of allocating backend services allowing developers to purchase on-demand services, which mean they only pay for services they use. With serverless developers do not have to deploy or maintain physical or virtual servers allowing them to develop and manage code execution.

CONTAINERS

Containers in the cloud have transformed from a development buzzword to an essential element in a business IT infrastructure. Containers offer a streamlined packaging process in which applications are virtualised from the environment in which they run. Containers are a streamlined, easy-to-deploy and secure method of implementing specific infrastructure requirements regardless of the environment is a private data centre or the public cloud.

CLOUD SERVICE MODEL

There are three main cloud service models in the public cloud Infrastructure-as-a-Service (IaaS), Platform-as-a-Service (PaaS), and Software-as-a-Service (SaaS). These models can be classified as "Host" – IaaS, "Build" – PaaS, "Consume" – SaaS.

Traditional IT	Infrastructure (as a Service)	Platform (as a Service)	Software (as a Service)
Applications	Applications	Applications	Applications
Data	Data	Data	Data
Runtime	Runtime	Runtime	Runtime
Middleware	Middleware	Middleware	Middleware
Operating System	Operating System	Operating System	Operating System
Virtualization	Virtualization	Virtualization	Virtualization
Servers	Servers	Servers	Servers
Storage	Storage	Storage	Storage
Networking	Networking	Networking	Networking

You Managed | Vendor Manages

IaaS – offers the most flexibility of the cloud models, allowing your organisation to deploy and consume complete infrastructure, scalability control, management and customisation control.

PaaS – a third-party vendor, provides the platform allowing you to deploy and run applications such as a SQL database. PaaS eliminates the need to install in-house hardware and software. The cloud provider would be responsible for managing the underlying infrastructure, and you would be responsible for maintaining the application configuration and data.

SaaS —allows you to access cloud-based services without installing new infrastructure quickly. The applications run on the vendor's cloud, which they control and manage. The service is paid on a licensed subscription basis.

There are many different models, strategies and concepts in this chapter that you must fully understand to develop a winning cloud strategy for your organisation. Only you can decide what strategy, service model or vendor is right for your organisation, and to make great decisions, you must have a strong cloud knowledge foundation.

- CHAPTER 3 -

Identify the Skill Gaps
Know your team's capabilities

"Without sharpen your weapon; standing on the battlefield would not increase your chance of winning."— Ankit Sahay.

Organisations migrating into the public cloud can achieve several benefits that include reduced costs, increased efficiency, flexibility, increased security and performance. Before embarking on your cloud journey, the organisation requires a precise and proper preparation. One aspect of this preparation is to assess the organisation readiness for cloud and evaluate the skills and experience necessary to go on their cloud journey. The organisation should have a clear vision of what skills and resources that are required to make the cloud journey a success. If the organisation underestimates the skills and resources required the journey to the cloud shall be slow, costly and lead to poor cloud adoption.

Migrating and running workloads in the cloud are no longer good enough. Your organisation needs to get the very best value from your cloud platform, cloud investment, keep ahead of your competitors and future-proof the business, to do this the organisation needs to hire and retain the best tech talent.

In today's environment, there is a shrinking number of certified and experienced employees available to meet the demand for public cloud.

"In this strong economic environment of significant business growth and record-low unemployment levels, the battle for talent is heating up as employees now have more bargaining power," said Matthew Shinkman, practise leader at Gartner. "As a result, talent is harder to find and even more difficult to keep."

CLOUD SKILLS ASSESSMENT

For a successful migration to the public cloud, the organisation must ensure that the team members have the correct skill set to implement the organisation's cloud strategy, workload migration, support and management of applications running in the cloud. The organisation, therefore, must execute an assessment of the team's ability and gauge their capabilities to have success in the cloud.

Once the assessment is completed and the gaps identified the organisation should address and fill those gaps over time. There are four strategies organisations can consider when addressing their skill gap:

Training – Upskilling existing staff to provide the required skill, using an internal or external trainer to upskill the team.

New Hires – One of the quickest methods to close the skills gap and bring new skills into the organisation.

Replacement – Replace existing employees with new employees that have targeted skills.

Outsourcing - Work with a cloud partner who has the capability and skills to help with your cloud journey. The organisation must identify which cloud roles are suited to be outsourced vs in-house roles, factors that may influence this decision are access to talent, business-critical systems and security concerns.

The technical skills gap assessment might reveal that the organisation may not have an adequate number of resources required to have a successful migration. The results can be used to inform the organisation to hire new employees and upskill the existing staff.

This stage of technical requirement analysis leads the organisation to identify how many resources are required, what new technical skills need to be developed, and what role an outsourcing partner shall play in the migration journey.

Assessing your team's ability and skills to develop your organisation's cloud strategy, migration plan and execute the migration is the first initial step in your cloud journey. Getting this assessment done early is essential, as you will be able to plan and make great decisions when migrating to the cloud.

IMPORTANT SKILLS FOR PUBLIC CLOUD

Public cloud is growing at a rapid rate and the skills required to fulfil this demand are in short supply. The organisation must understand the skill set needed to help on their cloud journey.

Technical Skills – The technical skills required for an organisation shall vary depending on what stage your organisation is at in its cloud journey, the amount of app development, management and the cloud vendor you choose.

Cloud Architecture – This is essential to develop the cloud roadmap of services required for the business, design the workload architecture and cloud service model.

Business Skills – Required to develop the business case for cloud migration, return on investment, the total cost of ownership and analyse cloud cost going forward.

Cloud Project Management – Cloud PM skills are essential to ensure cloud migration and cloud deployment projects are delivered on time and within budget.

Security Skills – Security skills are one of the most in-demand across the cloud. A deep understanding of security protocols, mandates, regulation and compliance is essential.

Application Development Skills – Strong demand for employees who can develop cloud and mobile applications across the cloud stack.

Contract Negotiations – The skills required to negotiate SLA's and understand the fine print of a vendor contract is important. To hold the vendor accountable if SLA's are not met and re-negotiate improved T&Cs.

CULTURE OF LEARNING

The public cloud is changing at a rapid speed and keeping pace; you should develop a culture of learning that is validated through certification. If the organisation promotes a culture of learning the workforce can quickly adapt to the pace of change within the cloud. Creating a culture of learning starts with the board and works its way down. Business leaders can fast-track this culture of learning by establishing a cloud centre of excellence within the organisation.

OUTSOURCING SKILLS

Outsourcing technical expertise should be a natural step for most organisations in the public cloud as they have effectively outsourced their storage, compute, database and other cloud resources. Once the organisation has completed and assessed the skills gap report, you may find that it is cheaper, quicker with less risk to outsource critical responsibilities to a cloud service provider.

Outsourcing will help the organisation bring in new skills faster with a fresh perspective and approach for cloud migration. The organisation must make sure that it evaluates the required skills very carefully before outsourcing. There is a high demand for cloud professionals; if the organisation is looking for a cloud partner, it must ensure that the Outsourcing partner has the right skills and experience that merges with the organisation requirements.

ASSESSING A CLOUD PARTNER SUITABILITY

Before you can assess the suitability of a cloud partner, you need to understand your organisations specific business goals, current technical skills and capacity. You should develop a checklist of requirements to evaluate potential cloud partners, their capabilities, experience and reliability you are going to entrust into them.

Financial health – does the cloud partner have the financial muscle to operate successfully throughout your transition to the cloud and beyond if required?

Certification – the cloud partner should have trained and experienced resources on the public cloud platform and technologies that you have identified to support your organisation in the cloud.

Governance – you need to look beyond the traditional IT governance model and ensure that your cloud partner has a mature cloud governance and operating model.

Standards – your organisation may have specific standards that it needs to enforce like ISO-27001, GDPR, PCI and HIPAA. When choosing a cloud partner, you should assess their ability to comply with those standards and the partner's ability to help your organisation implement best practices around those standards.

Technical capabilities – your cloud partner must have the technical skills and experience to implement your cloud migration and support you thereafter. Your cloud provider should have hybrid cloud capabilities, even if you don't plan to use this approach. Hybrid has distinct advantages that you may wish to exploit later.

Management – the cloud partner should have event and change management capabilities with proven systems and methodologies

SLA – the cloud provider should have SLAs specific to your cloud environment requirements. Have the ability to monitor performance against SLA guarantees.

Customer reference – One of the best ways to assess a cloud partner suitability is by talking to their customer's. They provide the most accurate real-world evaluation of ongoing performance.

Security – The cloud partner must have comprehensive security policies and procedures in place for controlling access to your data and applications. This should be well documented to demonstrate adequate security across IaaS, PaaS and SaaS.

Lock-in – You may find that after working with a cloud partner for a period that you are not a fit for each other. The process of moving from one cloud partner to another should be documented within the SLA and any financial risk of moving.

- CHAPTER 4 -

Cloud Centre of Excellence

Build momentum and best practice

"We need to internalize this idea of excellence. Not many folks spend a lot of time trying to be excellent." —— Barack Obama.

Cloud Centre of Excellence (CCoE) is a team which spearheads the introduction of cloud services into the organisation. The CCoE team champions the transformation process to the cloud environment, provides technical guidance, training and supports the organisation during the transition period to the cloud, ensuring each employee is on board. The CCoE team should have executive support to drive adoption, migrations, operations, set goals and priorities for the organisation, including target efficiencies, increased agility, governance objectives, project deadlines and new revenue opportunities for the organisation. The CCoE team is responsible for the introduction of new frameworks and structures within the organisation, standardising organisation processes, the management of disruption, and making sure that the organisation overcomes barriers during cloud adoption.

After the adoption of the cloud, the CCoE team will review the organisation change process and focus on continual improvement of cloud solution to meet the business objectives. The CCoE team is dedicated to cloud transformation and its responsible for research, cloud solution planning, and managing complex logistics of cloud solution adoption.

WHY DEVELOP A CLOUD CENTRE OF EXCELLENCE TEAM

Organisations move to the cloud when clear benefits are identified, and business objectives can be achieved through cloud technology; usually, this starts with a small group of employees.

In most cases, the idea for the cloud does not have the buy-in from the key stakeholders within the organisation; that's when you should start developing your CCoE team. CCoE team ensures that everybody within the organisation is involved and the cloud transformation information has reached all the organisation stakeholders. The CCoE team enables the accelerated adoption of the cloud within the whole organisation. Through the CCoE, the organisation is able to reduce risks and maximise the ability to achieve the benefits of cloud adoption. CCoE team is a cross-functional platform with different people of different skills; hence the cloud solutions adopted by the organisation through this team will be in line with the business objective and the organisation business goals.

For cloud adoption to be successful, all the entire organisation is needed on board before migrating any workloads; the CCoE enhances this by promoting the best practices and efficiency designed for the organisation culture. The CCoE team comes up with the automated policies, usage, analyse costs, performance, the security of the cloud environment, recommendations on cloud capacity planning, forecasting and modelling of the cloud solution. The CCoE makes sure that everybody within the organisation embraces the cloud culture and is ready to help the organisation streamline their processes to achieve its business objectives. To make the cloud migration smooth and successful, the organisation needs a well-staffed and equipped CCoE team

The CCoE team serves as the strong advocates' and champions of cloud adoption within the organisation, helping the organisation staff and stakeholders to be enthusiastic about the cloud. CCoE finds new ways of achieving the desired business goals and serves as the catalyst for innovation within the organisation. Through the strategies and the frameworks developed by the CCoE team, it will help the organisation to evolve and position itself for long term success.

The CCoE team helps the organisation to accelerate cloud adoption by driving the momentum of all the stakeholders, and the CCoE team develops frameworks that can be reused for cloud governance and adoption, The CCoE team manages the cloud knowledge and learning across the organisation, overseeing the cloud plan to align the cloud offering to the organisation strategy.

The CCoE team drives the organisation cloud maturity forward and sets the agenda for cloud solution adoption. The CCoE team also makes decisions regarding cloud architecture and processes.

The CCoE team has major responsibility for providing and setting the platform for successful cloud migration while encouraging collaboration among the stakeholders within the organisation. The CCoE team advise the organisation and implements the cloud solution by providing great thought leadership and hands-on technical support during the cloud journey.

HOW TO BUILD A CLOUD CENTRE OF EXCELLENCE TEAM

The CCoE team should be built well in advance before the organisation undertakes the decision to migrate the first workload. However, organisations can start with a cloud migration first without the CCoE team, and then introduces the CCoE team midway to provide governance and best practices. Once the organisation selects the CCoE team members, the evangelism of the cloud is established.

CLOUD CENTRE OF EXCELLENCE TEAM ROLES

The CCoE team member roles will depend on the size of the organisation and its cloud maturity. In a smaller organisation, one person may have responsibility for a number of functions like networking and infrastructure, whereas in larger organisations these roles will be separated out. The CCoE team should have the skills and ability to move fast and accelerate the successful migration to the cloud with high cloud adoption.

Leader: The CCoE should consist of a senior leader or someone from the top hierarchy of the organisation to provide direction and leadership for the business transformation. The CCoE leader shall be responsible for establishing, maintaining and promoting the CCoE team inside the organisation, leading collaboration across the organisation.

Cloud Architect: This person is responsible for designing the new cloud system to best practice, maximising performance, costs and taking full advantage of the cloud capabilities. The Cloud Architect comes up with the requirements that determine how the cloud system will work and provides guidance to the developers and engineers.

Project Manager: The person in this role is responsible for spearheading the team's project management and project execution. The PM is responsible for making sure that the team are aligned to the best practices and the accepted standards.

Operations Manager: During the cloud transition and migration, the CCoE team needs to understand the business processes, workflows and procedures of the organisation. A team member from the operations department is necessary for the CCoE team to provide advice and guidance on the organisation business processes. This person is responsible for guiding the configuration process and the cloud infrastructure deployment, this includes network architecture, access management, application security, monitoring, logging and billing.

Site Reliability Engineer: The person ensures that the services are reliable to the user's needs. The individual is responsible for latency, availability, performance, change management, efficiency, monitoring, capacity planning and emergency response. The individual focusses on the health of the implemented cloud solution to meet the business objectives.

Infrastructure Engineer: The CCoE team requires a member from the infrastructure team to advise on the current on-prem infrastructure and the new public cloud environment to deploy. They are hence helping the team to decide which cloud model to be implemented.

Network Engineer: The individual is responsible for developing and maintaining the cloud network infrastructure. The Network Engineer has responsibility for developing and designing enhancements that make the system run smoothly. Also makes sure that the network is safe and running efficiently through monitoring of performance.

Security Engineer: The security engineer is in charge of the security of the organisation infrastructure and applications in the cloud. This person's role is to advise the organisation on security best practice that meets the highest cybersecurity standards, advising on the security risks and vulnerabilities.

KEY FUNCTIONS WITHIN A CLOUD CENTRE OF EXCELLENCE TEAM

Adoption: The CCoE team is responsible for the adoption of the cloud. The roles and activities offered by the CCoE include accelerated adoption of the cloud through increased cloud feature usage, through the implementation of well-designed and secure cloud infrastructure.

The CCoE team encourages collaboration among the organisation stakeholders by creating and promoting the communication channels, defining the collaboration activities and making sure the collaboration barriers are minimized.

The team increases the awareness about the cloud solution by granting employees access to cloud information, encouraging and providing a platform for open communication in the organisation and empowering the employees to make decisions.

Governance: The CCoE team provide a governance role by providing cloud advisory and best practices. The team advise the organisation on the cloud methodology to be adopted for the successful transition into the cloud. The team advise the organisation on the cloud optimisation strategy, oversees the cloud utilisation in the organisation, improves data usage and management of the data. The team standardise the organisation processes and methodologies to achieve cloud adoption, and it incorporates the best methodologies. The team develops and oversee the framework for tools standardised across the functions of the organisation.

Knowledge management: The CCoE team manages the knowledge by serving as a knowledge management central point. The team is the central point for any queries concerning the cloud in the organisation, and the team supports the training development of the cloud. The CCoE team provides the learning culture within the organisation, encouraging continuous learning by developing a culture of knowledge and excellence. The team also provides thought leadership by developing cloud practices specific to the organisation processes and objectives, and the team also develops points of view on the organisation implementation of the cloud and the management of the creation of assets.

Operations: The CCoE team provides cloud management by monitoring the operations of cloud usage, the management of cloud permissions. The team also monitor the operations of the cost optimisation within the organisation by monitoring costs and managing the billing. The team oversees the operation of the metrics and Key Performance Indicators through identifying metrics, capturing and updating of the key performance metrics, reporting of the key performance metrics to the executive team and onboarding new members to the CCoE team. The team also provides cloud security by managing cloud permissions, managing access and identity of all users and by incorporating the security protocols needed in the cloud architecture.

Strategy: The team comes up with the strategy to make sure that the organisation meets its business objectives in the cloud. This is done by executing the cloud strategy, and the team prioritizes the initiatives and projects to be implemented, the team comes up with the modern cloud infrastructure technology and accelerating the go-to-market products and services. The team spearheads innovation within the organisation by adopting the new use cases in the cloud, through the championing of the technological innovations that will help the organisation to achieve its goals.

The team provides the integration of the organisation strategy; this includes the promotion of cross-functional business process integration and aligning the cloud strategy to the general organisation business strategy. The team provides the cloud program management in the organisation by coming up with the plan sprints and upgrades to the cloud solution and monitoring the access and identity in the cloud environment. Finally, the team provides strategic alignment by ensuring the business alignment and by communicating to the top organisation hierarchy in the adoption of the cloud strategy.

- CHAPTER 5 -

Cloud Strategy Options

Know where you are going and why

"We've had three big ideas at Amazon that we've stuck with for 18 years, and they're the reason we're successful: Put the customer first. Invent. And be patient." .— Jeff Bezos, CEO of AWS.

A great cloud strategy should address WHY your organisation should use the cloud, and WHAT does your organisation want to achieve by implementing the public cloud. I believe that true business competitive advantage is carved out at the strategic level and a cloud or digital transformation strategy gives your business a sustainable advantage if done well. The adoption of the public cloud has been on a steep incline as more and more organisations recognise its benefits for their long-term business goals.

A well-thought-out and planned cloud strategy are essential to the success of your business and journey to the cloud. Understanding the WHY and WHAT of your cloud strategy forms the core of your cloud strategy. A cloud strategy does not state the specific technologies or cloud model you should adopt.

In this chapter, I will discuss the key elements that your organisation will need to develop for their cloud strategy like cloud vision, principles and goals etc. I will also touch on several core cloud strategies for you to consider when planning your organisation cloud strategy.

CLOUD VISION

A clear cloud vision acts as the foundation for your public cloud strategy. I have seen public cloud deliver real cost-saving and agility to many organisations. All the successful organisations in the cloud have a clear vision for their business on how the public cloud will enable their strategy. If you dive right in and start delivering cloud services, there is a danger that cloud services delivered do not match business goals, expected value and benefits to the organisation. This misalignment can lead to poor cloud adoption, increased cost and lead to failure.

CLOUD PRINCIPLES

When the cloud vision has been completed, you should define your core cloud principles that are aligned to the cloud vision. The cloud principles are specific statements on how your team will implement the cloud vision. Some examples I have seen in other organisation of cloud principles are cloud-first, cloud-only, SaaS first, PaaS second and IaaS third, self-service model first, security over user experience and multi-vendor, to name a few. There is no right or wrong answer to what your organisation cloud principles should be. However, it should enable the delivery of the organisation cloud vision.

FOCUS ON USERS AND VALUE

Your cloud strategy should support all the different users within the organisation to enable productivity and drive innovation. Most organisations have it backwards when they choose a technology to drive business value instead of delivering value for users that drive technology choices. You should understand the value drivers to both internal or external customers and the underlying technology that shall support value creation.

BUSINESS GOALS

The cloud strategy should outline the business goals and the value creation to users and the organisation. The business goals shall change from organisation to organisation like reduce time to market, agility, monthly billing, scalability and reduced costs. Careful consideration should be given when selecting your goals in adopting a cloud service and how they will be measured.

WHY DEVELOP A STRATEGY

"Strategy without tactics is the slowest route to victory. Tactics without strategy is the noise before defeat." Sun Tzu

All organisations have a business strategy, either it's a known or unknown strategy but its far better to have a well thought out strategy. A great strategy will define the direction, goals and priorities for your organisation; the business strategy should also clearly define what the organisation does not do! "A strategy is necessary because the future is unpredictable." Robert Waterman

The strategy informs the leadership team on the direction of the organisation and what the team should work on first. Without a strategy, your team may work on tasks and projects with little value to the organisation success.

Moving your organisation to the cloud is a journey that can benefit the entire business, which may take many years. Organisations need to think strategically when planning their cloud journey, as there are many things to consider along the way.

MULTI-CLOUD STRATEGY

Up to 81% of organisation have adopted a multi-cloud strategy, sighting that one cloud provider does not meet their business and technical requirements. The organisation is choosing a multi-cloud environment as they see the value of expanding their cloud platform portfolio as a better method to improve customer and employee value.

Gartner VP analyst Michael Warrilow, said, "Most organisations adopt a multi-cloud strategy out of a desire to avoid vendor lock-in or to take advantage of best-of-breed solutions. We expect that most large organisations will continue to pursue this approach willfully."

Whether an organisation is planning on a multi-cloud strategy or not, you should consider implementing a multi-cloud monitoring and cost management platform. This approach shall future-proof your public cloud vendor decisions in the future, and if you acquire another business, you have the systems in place to manage a multi-cloud environment.

HYBRID CLOUD STRATEGY

A hybrid cloud strategy provides an organisation with strategic advantages to solve real business problems and take advantage of both types of cloud. By enabling both types of cloud across the organisation, the business can take advantage of both private and public benefits, streamline business functions, maintain control and protect sensitive data in the private cloud. A hybrid cloud strategy enables the movement of workloads with increased agility and additional options for data management. For most organisation hybrid cloud is the only option because of its greater flexibility.

The easiest way to describe a hybrid cloud is a mix of public, private and on-prem technology solutions that you can manage. There is no doubt that the hybrid is more complex to manage. However, a hybrid cloud offers the best parts of the public, private and on-prem solutions to address your organisation needs.

Gerry Gosselin, VP of Engineering, says applications and data gravity should drive your hybrid cloud strategy. "Some of our clients are simply looking to extend their data centre into the cloud for increased capacity or disaster recovery. Others choose specific applications to be in the cloud rather than on-premises. Not every application should or can be in the cloud, and not all data make sense to store in the cloud. That decision needs to be made on an application by application basis."

DEVELOPING A CLOUD STRATEGY

A good cloud strategy should address the WHY and WHAT of cloud adoption that enables business goals and drives customer value. You and your team shall have several discussions and debates whether to use IaaS or PaaS, SaaS or custom build a solution – should you adopt microservices and serverless technologies. Your team will get locked down in the benefits of each technology and, express a preference with the pros and cons of each option. When you choose a technology, this is not a strategy! The reality is that you will use them all at the same time, and the real question is how much of each shall we use.

CLOUD OPERATING MODEL STRATEGY

As more and more organisations transition towards the cloud, we are finding that little consideration has been given to how the organisation will operate in the cloud, where they continue to follow the same processes and practices as in a traditional data centre or on-prem scenario. A detailed Cloud Operating Model provides a holistic view of the future business state, providing the foundation across technology, people and processes allowing the business to execute its cloud strategy and deliver real value to their customers.

Most organisations have defined a classic IT operating model around traditional IT infrastructure support, processes and technology in a static environment. You cannot expect this traditional operating model to work in the cloud that is agile and continuously evolving. Only by evolving the current processes of managing an organisation's infrastructure and applications, the benefits of the cloud can be secured.

A common example of how organisations do not correctly understand the cloud operating model is when it comes to cloud costs and controls. In a traditional model, when a new server was required, the engineer would seek approval from their manager, a PO for that hardware would be created, and the purchase process would be kicked-off. The Hardware would arrive several days later, and the engineer would install the server on to the network. In today's cloud world, the engineer can just deploy or increase the spec of the resource without any prior approval.

DON'T GET CAUGHT UP IN THE HYPE

There is no doubt that the adoption of cloud services has driven cloud to be one of the fastest-growing technologies. CIOs and business leaders are under extreme pressure to adopt and maximise the benefits of the public cloud. Moving your Organisation to the cloud for the sake of it is the worst reason in the world to do so. The cloud offers benefits, including the enhanced reliability, flexibility, manageability and scalability. On the other hand of the coin is the dark side of the cloud if you are unprepared with underperformance, connectivity issues, cost overruns and operational control issues. However, CIOs should proceed and take advantage of the cloud with a well-thought-out digital transformation, cloud migration and adoption strategy.

CLOUD SECURITY STRATEGY

The confidence in public cloud security has grown over recent years with the larger providers, and the security management is the responsibility of each organisation to secure their data and applications in the cloud. It is important to align the organisation overall existing security strategy to the public cloud security strategy. The organisation must understand that they will need to modify their existing security to facilitate the reality of the cloud. The cloud security strategy should address the new security concerns with the cloud and address issues like GDPR, governance and compliance.

CLOUD EXIT STRATEGY

Every organisation that is moving workloads to the cloud should create a cloud exit strategy, sometimes referred to as reverse migration and unclouding. A cloud exit strategy outlines how an organisation can move out of the cloud. It is good practice to create a cloud exit strategy as it promotes planning and awareness of the risk that may require the organisation to roll back. The organisation cloud contract with its vendors is the best place to start in preparation for your exit strategy. The contract should have clear performance, integration and security KPIs that must be achieved by the cloud vendor. If these KPIs are not achieved, the cloud vendor should bear the cost of rolling your workloads back to the original state.

CLOUD FINANCIAL MODEL STRATEGY

Knowing the financial cost of moving and operating in the cloud is an essential part of your cloud strategy and will influence decisions the organisation will make. The financial strategy should involve operations and financial leaders to assess the cloud financial options and resolve potential issues like cost visibility, budgets per department or workload, cost controls and predictability.

CLOUD INTEGRATION STRATEGY

As organisations move more and more workloads to the cloud and with the ease of cloud adoption, organisations face a risk that user experience will suffer as different workload and vendors solutions do not speak or integrate with each other. The ability for the organisation to effortlessly transfer data in real-time is fundamental to the organisation success. The challenge for organisations is to integrate and manage business applications and data so that the experience is seamless for every user.

For an organisation to enable a seamless integration of data between applications, organisations are looking to third-party integration tool to enable this. This reduces data complexity and frees up valuable resources to focus on other issues.

- CHAPTER 6 -

Public Cloud Economics
Stop flying blind

"A budget tells us what we can't afford, but it doesn't keep us from buying it."
— William Feather

Your organisation journey to the cloud is a strategic investment in new technology, processes and operating model that shall enable your business strategy and goals. Most businesses assess the economic value of the cloud with a like for like between on-prem and cloud; however, this can be grossly misleading.

A better approach would be to examine the entire cost of the cloud infrastructure, licensing, management, financial model costs and any additional capabilities gained with the public cloud, speed to market and digital innovation.

WHAT IS CLOUD ECONOMICS?

Cloud economics refers to the business drivers, economics forces and structural issues concerned with benefits and costs of adoption of cloud by organisations. Cloud economics, in its simplest term, is dealing with the costs and benefits of the cloud.

Cloud economics help an organisation to measure and analyse the principles, benefits and cost of cloud computing before adoption. Cloud economics also concerns the economy inside the cloud, includes monetisation, billing, charging, products taxation and services offered inside the cloud.

Many organisations are challenged to deliver quality technology services and to reduce the costs of this service delivery hence the adoption of the cloud. But before migrating to the cloud, the organisation must make sure that it has determined how the cloud service will affect the organisation both in staffing needs and budgets. Through a cloud economic assessment by the organisation, the IT leaders will be able to weigh the costs and all the necessary requirements pertaining to the cloud infrastructure, management and security based on the organisations business goals.

One of the biggest advantages of the public cloud is the opportunity for an organisation to save costs on their IT environment. Public cloud provides the organisations with the ability to use infrastructure that is only required at that time, thus only paying for what resources are used.

The organisation will be using the consumption-based model, which increases the organisation innovation and has access to the best and latest technologies. The consumption-based cloud model is good, but it's not predictable; hence the need for cloud economics before adopting it. The organisation needs to balance between agility and innovation against the cloud cost. This can be achieved using the Total cost of Operation methodologies (TCO) to compare the operating costs of implementing the cloud service against the traditional data centre.

Comparing the costs, the complexity of maintaining and running a traditional data centre, cloud computing is better due to the reduced costs and increased efficiencies. In the cloud, organisations can implement a scalable platform: database technologies, low-cost storage, management and deployment tools. Cloud computing helps the organisation to achieve reduced costs and complexity, reduces time to market, increased innovation opportunity, adjust based on capacity demand and enhanced security.

Know the true cost of your organisation cloud, and do not get caught unprepared with overruns on your cloud budget. Organisations that successfully manage and control their cloud spend have policies, procedures, tools and automation implemented across their cloud platforms.

CALCULATING PUBLIC CLOUD COST

The cost and time required for an organisation to migrate workloads to the public cloud are usually underestimated. This is due to a lack of experience and knowledge within the organisation in planning and migrating workloads to the cloud. They are several proven steps an organisation can take to calculate the cost of migration and running in the cloud

1. Calculate current & future infrastructure costs:

    The organisation should calculate the direct and indirect cost of running their IT infrastructure, the issue we see is that organisations only assess what their current costs are and do not consider what costs are involved in maintaining them systems over time. The task is important to build a business case for cloud adoption and give a real cost comparison.

2. Calculate cloud Infrastructure costs:

    The three public cloud giants, AWS, Azure and GCP all have cloud infrastructure price calculator to help your organisation calculate costs. At this stage, most organisations make the mistake of calculating their resource costs incorrectly, due to underestimating resource requirements, the incorrect cloud service model and not adopting a cloud optimisation strategy. A common mistake that organisations overlook is the operating cost of running the original infrastructure and the new cloud infrastructure together. Until the workload migration is completed, your team will have to manage and support two different infrastructure at the same time.

3. Calculate Cloud Migration Costs:

This is the cost of moving your workloads and data to the cloud. This cost would include the cloud architect, engineer to move the workload and the project manager. The cost of migrating workloads to the cloud will depend on each individual workload and if it's a simple lift and shift or refactoring is required to take advantage of the cloud platform capabilities.

4. Calculate Cloud Operating Costs:

This is the cost of operating and running the cloud infrastructure. This should include any third-party tools used to monitor performance, control/manage costs and DR software. The labour required to support the new cloud infrastructure, training and upskilling of those resources should be calculated in the operating costs.

HARD TO FIND CLOUD COSTS

The public cloud offers significant cost benefits to an organisation that move workloads to the cloud. To reduce the financial impact of migration to the cloud, your organisation should calculate all the costs involved. However, there is some cloud cost that can be hard to find and be included in your overall cloud costs.

1.   Pre-Migration upgrades

Before migrating to the cloud, some application and database may be required to be upgraded to work in the public cloud.

2.   Third-party tool

To manage and maintain the organisation cloud infrastructure, you will need several third-party tools to monitor performance and issues, control and manage costs and dr.

3.   Poor cloud Implementations

Regardless if an organisation uses a third-party migration service provider or internal resource, a poor migration and implementation are going to cost a lot more to fix.

4.   Inefficient storage

Cloud storage is extremely cheap and fast to deploy, and that is one of the reasons organisations love cloud storage. On average organisations only utilise 50% of the storage they pay for in the cloud and typically deploy incorrect storage types which can be very costly.

5.   Bandwidth

Bandwidth usage can be forgotten or underestimated by the organisation when calculating the potential cloud cost. An organisation should take advantage of the bandwidth usage tool to give them a benchmark of the estimate bandwidth and costs.

ECONOMIC BENEFITS OF THE CLOUD

The public cloud is one of the best innovations within the tech industry in the last decade; organisations can now harness the economic, operational and staffing benefits.

Cloud services lowered the total cost of infrastructure since the organisation can pay for only what it has used. The organisation will have increased strategic flexibility that will help it to meet the market needs without having to put up the onsite infrastructure, through cloud computing the organisation is able to utilize a higher server utilization to achieve the business goals it also enhances the capacity planning and lowers unit per cost.

Economic benefits include reduced employees required by the organisation to manage the cloud infrastructure, and the cloud vendor provides the required infrastructure that's cheaper and faster to deploy.

Operational benefits include reduced cost, automation, increased storage, better use of Information technology staff and better mobility.

The consumer benefits include shorter deployment time, worldwide availability, no software installation and no maintenance needed, the service provider makes sure that the application is constantly updated and improved.

The service providers benefit includes a predictable revenue stream for the organisation, regular upgrades and ownership of the operating environment.

CLOUD RETURN ON INVESTMENT – ROI

ROI is a commonly used business term to define past and future financial gain from an investment. Most organisations miss the bigger picture when defining their organisation cloud ROI, focusing on the cost-saving of the cloud instead of calculating the value cloud can bring to the organisation. An organisation should include in their cloud ROI the advantage of the cloud like faster time to market, increased productivity, Opex model etc

CLOUD TOTAL COST OF OWNERSHIP – TCO

Cloud Total cost of ownership states what the organisation will spend after the adoption of the cloud solution. It includes the costs that will be required to run the cloud engine. The organisation must use the TCO model to evaluate what it will spend after the cloud solution is adopted by comparing the on-premise IT infrastructure and the cloud infrastructure to be implemented. This will give the organisation the best view of the total costs it will incur to migrate to the cloud environment. TCO will define organisation spending and savings while in the cloud.

CLOUD FINANCIAL MODEL – CAPEX V OPEX?

Capex is the traditional model for IT departments, and OpEx is the new model for cloud computing. The two can be used in a cloud environment and have different implications for costs and operational flexibility. The public cloud is known for its cost-savings as it does not require any upfront Capex payments. This is not always the most economical in cases where static IT equipment investment can be less expensive.

Capex – is an upfront expense to create long term benefits for the organisation, such as acquiring infrastructure for critical IT systems. This CAPEX investment in IT infrastructure ties up crucial capital within the organisation, which could be used for other business-critical projects. The maintenance cost of such CAPEX asset is considered a CAPEX cost, as it extends the life of the asset. When Capex assets go beyond one year, the organisation can benefit from depreciation with reduced taxes for the current year. The longer the asset last, the more the organisation benefits from depreciation and the greater the tax deduction.

Opex – is the organisation operating costs to run the business day to day, such as cloud services. The cloud OPEX model is a pay as you go structure where cost is based on what you consume. OPEX spend is tax-deductible and can be subtracted within the P&L to increase your net profit.

CAPEX V OPEX - SUMMARY

Moving to the cloud is a complex decision for organisations to make. There are so many technical decisions that an organisation need to get right, alongside making the right financial decisions. There are so many considerations when it comes to your cloud investment and the correct financial model for cloud expenditures.

To help you make great decisions about the financial options within the cloud here is easy to understand comparison chart that outlines the key differences between Capex an OPEX model.

Capex	OpEx
Upfront Lump payment	Ongoing monthly cost
Depreciates over 3 - 5 years	Accounted in the current year
Listed as equipment or property	Listed as operating cost
Tax deducted as asset depreciates over the years	Tax deducted in the current year
The long lead time of an asset	On-demand service
Can have waste	Purchase only what you need
TOC can be hidden	TOC transparent
Contract lock-in	Monthly Contract

- CHAPTER 7 -

Cloud Readiness Assessment

Assess your organisation readiness and
accelerate the journey to the cloud

"Preparation doesn't assure victory; it assures
confidence." - Amit Kalantri

One of the best exercises to prepare your organisation for moving to the cloud is to conduct a cloud readiness assessment. A cloud readiness assessment assists the organisation in answering key questions when embarking on their cloud journey like costs, risks, security, governance and resource requirements.

For most organisations, starting their journey to the cloud can be overwhelming, with several moving parts and multiple unknown risks. Although organisations understand the value and benefits of moving to the public cloud, they struggle to start and develop a roadmap to guide their team. The key to a successful migration is planning, and this starts with the organisation readiness, discovery, and assessments.

CLOUD WORKSHOPS

Cloud workshops are a great way to educate the organisation on the opportunity within the cloud—the different types of cloud services, cloud concepts and service model etc. Cloud workshops should identify business goals and initiatives that start to define the organisation cloud roadmap.

The objective of a well-run cloud workshop is to bring the key business and IT stakeholders together, enabling the organisation to make faster decisions and enhance cross-department collaboration.

Before holding a workshop, it would be a good approach to inform and educate the stakeholders with relevant information - giving the stakeholders time to prepare for the workshop, alongside gathering information from the stakeholders on their department. The organisation can collect workshop data via a questionnaire or survey, uncovering information like business strategies, business challenges, cloud maturity, Tier 1 apps, IT issues, security, operational etc. It is important to align the right people with the appropriate workshops.

There are several different types of workshops your organisation can benefit from depending on its cloud maturity and stage you are at in your cloud journey. Each workshop shall have its own unique goals and shall require a diverse skillset and input to be successful.

Cloud Overview Workshop - Discuss the business and technology requirements, what the cloud looks like today and in the future, and how the cloud could impact the business in a positive or negative way.

Cloud Migration Workshop – The workshop should guide the organisation through all the different migration strategies and consideration when migrating to the cloud. Identify the business drivers, planning, training, staffing and applications to be migrated to the cloud. The output from this workshop should be a high-level migration strategy for each workload, project resource requirements and plan to migrate the cloud.

Cloud Operational Workshop – The objective of this workshop is to understand and define how the organisation will operate the new infrastructure in the cloud. The team should discuss the end to end management of the entire IT infrastructure across the organisation and identify if the current IT operations model fits within a cloud environment. The output from this workshop should be a high-level strategy to manage and operate on-prem and cloud infrastructure with best practice and efficiency.

Cloud Architect Workshop – The purpose of this workshop is to discuss business-critical workload designs against best practices. This workshop guarantees the workloads are secure, reliable, cost-effective with the best security, performance and optimisation to maximise the workload infrastructure, configuration and costs.

Cloud Economic Workshop – It is important to have all the key stakeholders, including the financial team, to understand the costs of the cloud. The workshop team should discuss the business value of the cloud, ROI for each workload, budgets and a plan if cloud cost goes over budget.

Cloud Application Workshop – The workshop should identify the different workloads in the organisation, the workload suitability for the cloud and its priority in the migration journey.

Cloud Security Workshop – The workshop should educate stakeholders about the security risks and challenges operating in the cloud, identifying security best practice for multi-cloud, hybrid-cloud, workloads and on-prem IT infrastructure. The workshop should discuss how the current IT security strategy aligns with the new cloud environment and its challenges.

Cloud Governance Workshop – The workshop should define how cloud infrastructure, costs, applications and data are secure, compliant and are adhering to best practices. The workshop should outline how guidelines, policies, and processes are going to be implemented, managed and monitored to ensure compliance across the organisation.

Workshops – The best way to educate your organisation on the benefits of the cloud. It is also a superb method to gather information from key stakeholders and get their valuable insight.

CLOUD READINESS ASSESSMENT FRAMEWORK

The goal of a cloud readiness assessment framework is to ensure that the organisation is aligned to the business goals, identify the complexity of moving to the cloud and help with the organisation adoption of cloud services. A mature cloud readiness assessment framework assists organisation across three core areas of technology, process and people to prepare the organisation for their cloud journey

TECHNOLOGY - CLOUD READINESS ASSESSMENT FRAMEWORK

A technology readiness assessment is a process of assessing workloads and data suitability for the cloud. The technology readiness assessment shall identify the impact and challenges of move individual workloads to the cloud, and the steps required for a smooth migration.

After completing a technology readiness assessment, you should understand your current environment and any issues that need to be resolved before starting your migration. You now can estimate budget and a set of requirements to be completed before the migration. The technology readiness assessment should include

- Phase 1: Portfolio Analysis

Application Portfolio Assessment – This involves reviewing all the organisation's applications, mapping applications to departments and groups of users, the complexity of moving to the cloud, the technology used, interaction with other systems, application usage and its fit for purpose.

Infrastructure Portfolio Assessment – reviewing all you're on-prem servers, both physical and virtual, databases, storage types and quantity of storage. This should also include technology used like OS, programming languages, database types, versions, security posture, performance requirements, business logic, data governance and availability.

Dependence Assessment – The goal of dependency assessment is to identify how applications interact and depend on each other to function - assess the impact if something changes. Not all application dependencies are easy to spot, and many migrations run into significant
problems due to this oversight.

There are several cloud vendors and third-party solutions that can automate the application readiness assessment. I highly recommend that your organisation use one of these solutions alongside a manual readiness assessment.

- Phase 2: Suitability and Placement

Suitability Assessment – One of the most important factors to consider before moving to the cloud is which workloads are suitable for the cloud. There are several applications that increase the business value when migrating to the cloud and other applications which are not suitable and bring no business value. We have helped organisations around the world to assess suitability using these four headings

1. Assess the business suitability of the application for the cloud - governance, compliance, security standards, business continuity, GDPR, time to market and user experience.

2. Financial – What is the ROI for that application in the cloud. Assess the hosting cost, licencing, management, operations and optimisation options.

3. Technical – Is the application technically feasible for the cloud - performance, legacy technology and interaction requirements.

4. Functional – Assess functional of the application in the cloud-like security requirements, migration complexity and dependency mapping.

Placement Assessment – Your placement strategy is a key factor in the success of your cloud migration, deciding where to run workloads – on the public, private, on-prem or hybrid cloud. The placement strategy needs careful thought as workloads have different performance requirements. Also, the lifecycle stages of your workloads shall change. The decision to develop an application in the public cloud at this stage of the application lifecycle may be the perfect decision due to speed of development, deployment and scalability.

After the application has been developed, the speed of deployment and scalability is now not a priority, and the cost of running the application may be the highest priority which may affect where you locate that workload.

A placement strategy is an ongoing assessment as your business grows and priorities change, getting the placement strategy wrong can increase costs with a misalignment of business goals.

PROCESS - CLOUD READINESS ASSESSMENT FRAMEWORK

The biggest challenge organisation shall face when migrating to the cloud is to understand the impact on their day to day operations. The process readiness assessment examines how the organisation operates and how the business processes may be impacted.

Moving to the cloud involves change; a lot of process changes within the organisation and business units. The underlying technology change is less complex compared to the business and operational changes required.

Business processes may be negatively affected when migrating to the cloud. The objective of a process assessment is to understand each process in the organisation and to determine if the improvement is required in the cloud. Some process shall migrate to the cloud without any issues while other processes will require innovative thinking and will change dramatically.

PEOPLE - CLOUD READINESS ASSESSMENT FRAMEWORK

Migrating to the public cloud will change the way people operate and work. With any type of change within an organisation, you shall face resistance regardless of the business benefits like faster time to market, stability or to enable a mobile workforce. The organisation, IT team, shall be one of the first groups of employees to be reviewed in the people readiness assessment. Every employee will have different tolerance for change and upskill period.

- CHAPTER 8 -

Cloud Integration

Connect your applications and data across the organisation in a single cohesive manner

"With the cloud, individuals and small businesses can snap their fingers and instantly set up enterprise-class services." ~ Roy Stephan, Founder and CEO of PierceMatrix

In simple terms, cloud integration involves bringing together multiple cloud environments across the different cloud service model like IaaS, PaaS and SaaS, so that those applications and data can operate as a single IT system within the organisation. Organisations can achieve high levels of application and data integration with cloud integration and automation tools. Cloud integration is a set of tools and technologies that addresses the age-old problem of business data silos.

Any organisation moving to the cloud must have an integration strategy from the very start. Most organisations don't use the cloud as a single homogenous but as a hybrid model of on-prem, public and private clouds. Cloud services like Office 365 or HubSpot are at risk of being a data silo, unconnected to any other systems in the organisation. Unless the organisation considers each cloud service as part of a wider integration plan and take steps to combine the data in an orchestrated way, it will be hard to gain efficiencies or insights.

TYPES OF CLOUD INTEGRATION

Cloud integration can connect the cloud to cloud systems including SaaS, PaaS, IaaS and cloud to on-prem with a mix of any of the above. Data and applications are the two different types of cloud integration.

Data integration: Has the objective of synchronising and sharing data between different data stores or repositories. Data can be transformed, transferred and processed through data integration.

Applications integration: Has the objective of connecting multiple applications to share requests, commands and other functionality to enable business workflow processes. This is much more than sharing data; it connects the applications to work as one system across the organisation.

CLOUD INTEGRATION CHALLENGES

Organisations are consuming and adopting cloud services at an accelerated rate to maximise IT budgets. Application and data integration presents a real challenge for organisations, especially in a hybrid cloud that has a requirement to connect and transfer between on-prem and cloud systems.

Data Security: This is the key concern for organisations when moving to the cloud, connecting data between different systems and infrastructure adds complexity to the security concerns. Organisations that fail to address application and data security requirements have the potential to be very damaging and expensive. Data integration within a hybrid model such as on-prem and cloud that transfers data between systems, organisations need to identify and solve security vulnerabilities and security risks that are unique to the hybrid model.

Flexibility and Scalability: Data integration projects connect data between SaaS, PaaS and IssS, which add complexity and require multi scenarios to solve the data integration challenge. Data integration solutions need to be flexible to work across the different cloud service model allowing data transfer to work in both directions. Alongside this, the data integration solution must have the ability to scale as the organisation's data integration requirements grow with increased endpoints.

Operational Impact: With data transferring with ease across your hybrid cloud environment, the demand place on your monitoring and data change increases the load on these systems which can cause them to slow down across the entire operational systems. The demand placed on engineers to monitor and resolve data integration issues shall also put extra strain on your team's capacity and ability to deal with other issues inside the organisations.

Closed APIs: Most SaaS providers offer out of the box API connections into the data and application to address the cloud integration challenge. However, out of the box APIs can limit integration options and the ability of organisations to manage the data integration and flow that best suits their needs.

Data Explosion: There is no doubt that our data footprint has exploded with a mind-blowing quantity of data. Organisations need to ensure that they can scale to meet the storage requirements and only pay for what they use. Without proper management, the cost of data storage can very quickly become very expensive.

IPAAS

Integration platform as a service (iPaaS) is a cloud solution the enables organisations to host, develop and integrate data and applications. IPaaS provides organisations with a quick, simple and standardised approach of connecting data, applications, services and processes across the different clouds and on-prem environment. Integration projects are cheaper and quicker to implement when an organisation use IPaaS solutions as there is no hardware to purchase, no installation of IPaaS costs and no maintenance. Organisation pay for IPaaS is a subscription-based model.

ADVANTAGES OF IPAAS

As organisations quickly adopt cloud services, they are struggling to connect the different data silos and applications to provide a seamless business process workflow across the organisations. IPaaS tools are providing the solution for organisations to solve their data integration challenges, and IPaaP brings many advantages which we shall discuss below.

Increase Speed: The primary advantage of IPaaS is the speed at which your team can implement cloud integration projects. IPaaS can seamlessly connect with multiple applications and data store in a standardised approach. All the integrations programs and APIs can be accessed from a central location, the iPass platform.

Security: With the risk of potential data and application security breaches growing, organisations can reduce this security risk by implementing IPaaS solutions. IPaaS solutions have the highest security standards with real-time intrusion alerts and fraud detection that reduces the risk of a data breach

API Management: The IPaaS platform gives organisations a single portal to manage all their APIs. The organisations are able to develop and manage APIs in a reusable approach that saves time and improve team API management.

IPAAS SOLUTION FEATURES

Integration Flexibility: The IPaaS platform needs to work across the public, private, hybrid cloud and on-prem infrastructure. The IPaaS solution should integrate applications to applications, mobile apps and internet of things.

Ease of use. The IPaaS platform should have an easy to use portal and management interface. The IPaaS should have a graphic solution that will help engineers visualize and automate the integration workflow.

Security Access: Control and managed user access to cloud and on-prem within the IPaaS platform.

Out of the Box: The IPaaS platform should have pre-built integration connections as standard to the most popular and widely used applications like HubSpot, Salesforce etc.

- CHAPTER 9 -

Cloud Migration Strategy

Improving the organisation chances of a
successful migration to the cloud

"All you need is the plan, the road map, and the
courage to press on to your destinations." - Earl
Nightingale

C loud migration strategy is the organisation plan
to migrate applications and data to the public
cloud from an on-premise or datacentre
environment. A cloud migration strategy is important
since it helps the organisation to find the most efficient
way of migrating data and applications before going
live.
Organisations that have a documented migration
strategy to the cloud have a greater chance of success
compared to those organisations that migrate workloads
on an ad-hoc basis.

For an organisation to identify if a business workload is
suitable to be migrated to the public cloud, it first
evaluates that workload performance, security
requirements, service model and many other criteria to
determine its suitability for the cloud. To be successful
in the cloud, organisations need to develop repeatable

processes to enable their team to move securely and with speed to the cloud, ensuring a lower cost of ownership.

When planning your cloud journey, it's important to create a cohesive methodology strategy, taking advantage of the public platform capabilities and internal resources.

Organisations should develop their cloud methodologies with the proven and tested processes to solve issues in moving and operating in the cloud. A cloud methodology provides a list of detailed steps to overcome and accomplish the organisation's goals.

The migration methodology below includes 8 phases; however, not each workload migration will use each phase. The approach organisation should take is to review the below migration methodology and tweak it for their own business needs.

CLOUD MIGRATION METHODOLOGY

Phase 1: Discovery

- Audit of current hardware infrastructure
- Workload analysis audit
- Audit of security
- Compliance review
- Application dependence mapping
- DR and backup Audit
- Workshops

The first step in the Migration Methodology begins with understanding and discovering the current IT landscape, including hardware, data, workloads, Security, dependency, compliance and governance. The two approaches organisations can use to discover their current IT infrastructure is to either use an auto-discover solution or manually discover workloads that may consist of surveys, audits, workshops to document the different attributes of the landscape. We have found that organisations will use both methods to discover your current IT position, ensuring that the team do not miss anything at this phase.

Phase 2: Plan

- Develop a migration strategy
- Infrastructure architecture (compute, storage)
- Network architecture
- Security architecture
- DR architecture
- Integration architecture and plan
- Migration plan

Now that your organisation has a full picture of the IT environment and have decided to migrate to the cloud, the question is, how do we get there? The key to getting workloads to the cloud is in the planning and preparation.

For each workload, the team will need to define the migration strategy, define the suitability, placement, complexity, cloud service model, integration and security requirements. The workload architecture is designed at this phase, including network, compute, storage, backup, DR, monitoring and maintenance to support the workload in the cloud.

Phase 3: Proof of concept testing

- Run POC migration
- Execute UAT
- Identify workload risks

The proof of concept is important to determine how the workload will perform in a cloud environment. The POC is a critical step to identify unknown risks and allows the organisation team to solve these unknown risks and improve the overall workload performance.

Phase 4: Build

- Deploy infrastructure, networks and security
- Configure Infrastructure
- Network implementation
- Security implementation

The build phase of an organisation cloud infrastructure is froth with many unknown risks that can be overcome by experience and planning. The organisation migration team should have strong technical knowledge for how to deploy and configure infrastructure, networks and security as part of the build phase.

Phase 5: Migrate

- Communicate plan and schedule
- Execute a workload migration plan

- Migrate workloads to the cloud
- Install the application in the cloud
- Run your migration on applications and data

After all the weeks and months of creating the cloud strategy, planning and ensuring all the required prerequisites are in place, the workload migration to the public cloud should be a non-event. The organisation migration team will have a detailed plan in place to move groups of workloads to the cloud. The migration team will use both automated and manual methods to migrate workloads to handle the different operating systems, hypervisors, applications and data within your organisation.

Phase 6: Integrate

- Integrate application data and APIs
- Install monitoring, backup and DR

Organisations need the ability for their workloads to communicate and transfer data in real-time between SaaS, PaaS, IaaS and on-prem workloads. Users expect applications to be interconnected with a fully automated workflow to enable productivity efficiency. Workload operating in isolation with slow and expensive data transfers adds little value to the organisation.

Organisations must also integrate monitoring and management, backup and DR solutions to enable them to support and manage the workloads in the cloud.

Phase 7: Validate

- Validate workload and data functionality
- Validate workload performance
- Validate security
- Validate integrated services such as monitoring, backup and DR

This is one of the most important stages within the process as this outcome will determine if the workload goes into cloud production or not. Each workload should have its own validation criteria for success in the cloud. This may be down to application performance, user experience, agility or scalability. The organisation validation team shall validate if the infrastructure and workload meet functional, Security, reliability, integration & performance requirements. The technical team shall identify issues and make recommendations to resolve those issues, while the operational team will validate integration, such as monitoring and DR.

Phase 8: Operations Hand-Off

- The transition from the Migration team to the support team

Once the migration team has completed the workload migration to the public cloud, the handover to the operational team can occur. The migration team should be available to provide early care support to the operational team.

Phase 9: Optimise

- Optimise workload costs and performance
- Review and optimise workload design
- Review security best practices and improvement

Optimisation is an ongoing process to reduce cost, increase the performance and security of the workload. The technical team should create a roadmap for the organisation to convert workloads and optimise them to take full advantage of the cloud platform like using PaaS.

Phase 10: Decommission

- Uninstall original workload
- Delete data
- Destroy data hard drive
- Server shutdown and disposal

The final step in the migration methodology is to decommission physical and virtual asset and erasure data. The cloud migration plan should have a detailed list of all assets.

TYPES OF WORKLOAD MIGRATIONS

Organisations have several options when it comes to migrating workloads to the cloud, and it is not a one size fits all. Each migration strategy has its own pros and cons, depending on the workload and target environment.

My team and I have used all the workload migration strategies below to move workloads of all types to the three major public cloud vendors.

-        Rehosting - The approach involves shifting the exact current environment to the cloud. The organisation copy-pastes its on-premise environment to the cloud without making any changes. Organisations who got no long-term dreams of enjoying the benefits of cloud computing are well suited to use the rehosting approach.

-        Replatforming - This approach is the same as the rehosting approach but with some adjustments made by the organisation to optimise the cloud landscape. The application of core architecture remains the same. It's the best strategy for companies that need cloud computing for improved system performance.

-        Repurchasing - This approach, the organisation moves the workload to the new cloud environment such as SaaS. This can be the quickest, simplest and with the least-risk of operating workloads in the cloud. The organisation directly consumes applications from cloud vendors like outlook or Gmail.

-        Refactoring - The Refactoring cloud migration strategy the organisation rebuilds the applications from scratch. This approach is best when the organisation is leveraging on the cloud capabilities which are not available in the existing on-premise environment; an example is serverless computing. The approach is the most expensive cloud migration strategy but its compatible with the future technology versions.

- Retiring – This strategy involves identifying workloads that the organisation do not require and can be turned off without affecting the migration plan.

- Retaining - This strategy involves the organisation not migrating workloads into the cloud until it finds the cloud makes sense to do so.

CLOUD BEST PRACTICES FOR WORKLOAD MIGRATIONS

Public cloud workload migrations can be complex, and there are many good and bad practices when planning and executing a migration strategy. We shall discuss some of the best practices when migrating workloads to the cloud.

Document a clear Migration Strategy - the organisation should have a clear cloud migration strategy which identifies the company's business motives and the cloud migration use cases. The best migration strategy for the organisation is to migrate in phases by moving the less critical workloads, or the organisation can have a pilot project in the cloud to feel how the cloud will impact its business hence giving the organisation confidence of migrating fully to the cloud environment.

Develop cloud governance framework - a concern about moving to the cloud is security and compliance, creating a clear cloud governance framework will help the organisation to migrate to the secure cloud environment. The cloud governance framework should be well documented with clear policies and rules to secure the applications and the data in the cloud. A clear cloud governance document will define the roles, structure, policies, responsibilities, objectives, measures, principles and decision framework.

Optimise organisation Network - The organisation should first adopt an internet connection to enhance faster access to applications and data. The organisation can adopt the azure express service, which enables the organisation network to connect directly to azure hence making it faster. The organisation can also get faster internet connectivity from an internet service provider.

Early staff training - The organisation should train the staff earlier before the cloud migration so that they can have cloud expertise ready to move the organisation to the next stage. Early staff training enables the staff to adapt to the new approach and ways of running business processes in a different and smart way. The team can be trained in phases of cloud computing technology.

Automate processes - Organisation should make sure that the processes are automated to avoid downtime and disruption of services during cloud migration. Automation speeds up the migration process and lowers the risk and costs.

Cloud Usage Monitoring - The organisation should monitor cloud usage so that the organisation can control the budgets. The organisation can use a centralized dashboard to identify the different cloud service running instances. The organisation should also monitor the cloud usage for security and compliance so that it can collect the logs from the databases, and system to ensure that the required information security best practices are met.

CLOUD MIGRATION CHECKLIST

The purpose of a cloud migration checklist is to walk you through the steps to plan and start your journey to the cloud. For a successful cloud migration, you will need repeatable steps and actions that are carried out for each workload.

1. Start with your people – It's important from the start that you're engaged early with key stakeholders inside your organisation and get their support and buy-in.

2. Strategy First – Develop your cloud strategy, business goals, objectives and workload priorities for moving to the cloud

3. Cloud Readiness – Identify and document all applications on-prem servers, applications and dependency. Assess each workload readiness to be migrated to the cloud.

4. Costs – Calculate what it will cost to migrate the workloads, cloud resources and support costs. Estimate savings for running in the cloud.

5. Assess Skills gap – Analyse your current teams' skills to support the cloud strategy and future skills requirements. Identify outside partners that can help you in the planning and

implementation of the cloud strategy.

6. Migration Options – There are six commonly used migration options which you should know. Each workload within your application stack shall require its own unique migration option depending on its requirements.

7. POC – Run a POC for several workloads to assess the migration complexity, performance and potential costs for the cloud.

8. Workload Migration – After successful POC to the cloud, migrate all other workloads to complete your journey to the cloud.

9. Decommission – Once the workloads have been migrated to the cloud decommission the on-prem applications and systems.
.

10. Optimise – After the migration has been completed, you should continue to optimise and reduce cloud costs.

CLOUD MIGRATION CHALLENGES

As organisations seek to maximise their IT budgets, cloud plays an important part. Adopting cloud services can cause issues if not implemented correctly, and below we discuss the major challenges.

Data security: Organisations adopting the public cloud must manage their own security. Under the shared responsibility model, the organisation is responsible for the security of their VMs, applications and data. The organisation needs to secure the data and use encryption to meet compliance. The companies also must invest in security tools such as antivirus, malware protection and secure gateways so that they can protect the data from cyber-attacks.

Downtime: During the cloud migration, organisations may face downtime due to systems been required to be offline to execute the migration. This issue can be solved by the organisation implementing hybrid cloud, proper backups and a well-planned workload migration strategy.

Data loss: While the organisations are migrating to the cloud, the company data is at risk, as the data can be accessed by unauthorized personnel. The organisation must make sure that it minimizes data security by implementing the best cloud security controls, such as application encryption and access control.

Resource management: The organisation needs to train the IT personnel on cloud usage. The organisation may need to introduce new IT roles to change business operations.

Interoperability: The organisation existing applications do not communicate properly with the new cloud environment hence making it hard for the organisation's processes to run smoothly.

Lack of cloud expertise: With the increased adoption of the cloud and the advancement in technologies, organisations are migrating faster than ever to the cloud. Due to the advanced technology and cloud tools, an organisation needs well-versed expertise. IT staff are costly, and organisations need a lot of resources to run the cloud operation.

Bandwidth Cost: Organisations operating and running intensive applications and data in the cloud may have higher operating costs due to bandwidth requirements. All the three major public cloud vendors charge for data that leaves their cloud data centres, alongside this organisation may require a private dedicated line from their office to the cloud data centre.

CLOUD ARCHITECTING METHODOLOGY

A cloud architecture methodology is a repeatable process that organisations can use to architect best practice solutions in the public cloud. The methodology may change from organisation to organisation but to have a structure and process in place leads to better and cheaper cloud solutions—an example of a cloud architecture methodology.

Phase 1: Functional Architecture - Create a high-level functional Architecture design for the workload, identifying application functions, interactions and cloud platform components.

Phase 2: Operational Architecture - Create an operational model for that functional workload requirement like backup, disaster recovery, scalability, high availability, application monitoring, infrastructure management and platform components.

Phase 3: Resource Analysis - Define the workload performance requirements and benchmark for each workload. Identify the cloud resources needed on the platform for optimal workload performance.

Phase 4: Deployment Architecture - Develop the migration strategy of moving the workload to the cloud. The migration strategy shall depend on the outcomes of the above steps. The workload may need to be re-factor to enable PaaS components or large compute requirements.

Phase 5: Cost Analysis - Estimate the running costs of the workload in the cloud including backup, DR and any other platform solutions which support that workload. You should also estimate costs when the workload is optimised, like using a reserved instance.

Phase 6: Validation – The workload architecture, costs, migration strategy, resources and operation model should be validated before any workload is moved to the cloud. Many organisations have established an Architecture Review Board (ARB) or outsourced this function to a third party.

CLOUD ARCHITECTE REVIEW BOARD (ARB)

The cloud architecture review board (ARB) purpose is to ensure the workload architecture aligns with the organisations' strategy, goals and objectives. The ARB ensures that technical standards, policies and cloud principles are adhered to. Creating an ARB is a great way to enable architecture debate and ultimately end up with a better-architected solution.

When establishing an ARB, you should look for a broad range of skills from across the organisation. The ARB should have a diverse skillset from infrastructure engineers, network engineers, security engineers, operations and compliance. Each member of the ARB should have a well-defined role such as the security engineer should challenge the security of the workload, and the operations manager challenges how that workload will operate in the cloud.

When the ARB team has been created, set up a weekly meeting to sit down and review the proposed solution designs, the engineer or cloud architect who proposed those design should sit in front of the ARB and present the design. The role of the ARB here is to challenge all aspect of the design with the objective of improving the overall design.

- CHAPTER 10 -

Cloud Governance
Stay in control of your organisation

"Good corporate governance is about 'intellectual honesty' and not just sticking to rules and regulations, capital flowed towards companies that practiced this type of good governance." - Mervyn King

Cloud Governance is an agreed set of processes and policies to manage security, access, architecture, budgets, technology, cloud operations and compliance across your cloud environment. Moving to the cloud affects the roles of the employees, responsibilities and the processes of the organisation.

Cloud governance establishes the guidelines for organisations to operate in the cloud and reduces the risks. Without an established cloud governance model organisation may face many of these common problems: stalled projects, budget overruns, non-compliance, misalignment with the organisation objectives, incomplete risk assessment, poor adoption and continuous policy exception.

THE IMPORTANCE OF CLOUD GOVERNANCE

Cloud governance is important for organisations as it helps to reduce the risk of data loss, non-compliance with standards, aligns cloud spend with business goals and promotes innovation. Organisations need to reassess their cloud governance strategy to take full advantage of the cloud, like speed to market, cost savings and agility. The key to cloud governance lies in the automation of your processes in the cloud. With automation, you can enforce policies, budgets and compliance across your organisation.

Cloud Governance improves cloud resource management: With the best practices developed by different service providers like AWS, Azure and GCP effective cloud governance helps the organisation to manage multiple tenants, different resources and workloads across multiple platforms

Cloud Governance does away with shadow IT: Through cloud governance, the best framework is developed on how the organisation will work and how employees will access the cloud resources. Each employee will have access and membership to the required resources inhibiting the employees from using other resources to meet their mandate hence improving the security of the organisation data and processes.

Cloud Governance reduces the risk in the cloud: There are varied risks of operating in the cloud that includes data exposure, noncompliance with the best practices and cost overruns. Having cloud governance in place the organisation is able to ensure that the cloud accounts have proper security controls to keep them private and secure, the cloud resources are used in compliance with the existing regulations like HIPPA and others, and the organisation is able to control the spending so that the set limits are not exceeded.

CLOUD GOVERNANCE MATURITY LEVELS

Every organisation will be at a different level of cloud governance maturity. The goal of the cloud governance team is to assess their organisation cloud governance maturity level and create a roadmap to mature this. There are five maturity levels, as seen below.

• Level 1&2: Organisations have not addressed cloud computing risks.

1. Ad Hoc: The organisation has not set the governance processes. The organisation is unaware of the importance of managing the risks of cloud computing. The issues if they happen are solved in ad hoc fashion.

2. Initial: There are some cloud computing risk management processes in place. The organisation is aware of the cloud computing risk management benefit, but it's not implementing risk management.

• Level 3: at this level, the business organisation has formalised the cloud computing risk assessment. The organisation has made sure all risk assessment has been shared with everyone, and everyone understands it.

3. Defined: The organisation has a formal and well-defined cloud governance process that addresses the cloud environment risks and its implemented across the organisation. The organisation has organised and implemented a training program for managers to make sure that they have appropriate knowledge about cloud computing risks and how the risks should be mitigated.

• Level 4&5: at these levels, the organisation has included the key stakeholders and have acknowledged them. The organisation also has developed continuous process development.

4. Managed: The organisation has defined cloud computing, and the risk management associated with it is measurable, and process goals are implemented. The established processes include identification, assessment and the response to the potential risks. The organisation has also identified the strategies and risk mitigation processes.

5. Optimised: The organisation has implemented a comprehensive risk management plan of cloud computing and the associated measures enacted. The organisation has a developed,

continuous improvement process to enhance performance.

The foundation of cloud governance is a well-defined set of policies for the cloud environment that sets the standards for operating and compliance. Organisations should define what areas they may struggle to govern and start developing policies for these areas first.

CHALLENGES OF CLOUD GOVERNANCE

Organisations face major challenges in the cloud and governance is one of those challenges. Well defined governance will ensure that standards are met in the cloud and operate within agreed policies and procedures. Proper governance will ensure that the cloud services maintained, controlled and enable the organisation's strategy. The below challenges are some of the most common we have come across.

•   Compliance to laws and standards: the data located on the cloud must be protected to meet the business and legal requirements

•   Hard to estimate cloud computing risks: the inability to estimate the risks of cloud computing, the organisation are unable to assess the risks facing cloud computing and the lack of a holistic approach to mitigating them.

• Consequences of changing services: the change of cloud computing service will lead to unexpected results if the services are not well defined. The unexpected access will lead to major business loss.

• The uncertainty or no clear set of rules of who is responsible or accountable for protecting and safeguarding sensitive information / confidential information stored in the cloud.

• Information Technology is out of the loop when business organisation come up with decisions on the cloud resource usage.

• The IT personnel and functions in the organisation are not confident about all the cloud resources being used.

• The organisation supports the importance of encryption, but it's not implemented in protecting applications.

• The inability of the organisation to control how its employees and third-party stakeholders handle sensitive company data makes compliance difficult to achieve.

• Most organisation employees use cloud applications without having appropriate security measures in place, such as basic security training.

- The organisation allows a third party to access sensitive data stored on the cloud without having security reinforced like multi-factor authentication.

- The organisation dynamics affect cloud governance due to the introduction of new ways to build, test and release software. The new software will need new rules and new operating procedures.

- As data and systems are integrated, an increase in security and compliance is required across the cloud environment. The organisation must come up with new ways for measuring productivity, quality and service levels of the cloud solution hence an effect on the cloud governance.

- The development of cloud governance must be able to understand current accounting and financial model guidelines so that the best policy for cloud costing is developed. The operating expenses must be established and monetarization of acceptable data policies.

- Capacity to Adapt to change - The cloud governance team must be well adept with the business lines, operational functions and the technology practices of data privacy, data residency observatory rules and intellectual property. The policies should be developed on how the new technologies will affect the options and the speed of evolution.

BUILD YOUR ORGANISATION CLOUD GOVERNANCE

Organisations can manage their cloud infrastructure through a combination of people, process and technology. For organisations to securely and effectively operate in the cloud, a governance team is required to deal with cloud issues. The governance team will have oversight across the whole business and deal with cloud issues that may affect compliance and best practices etc. Below we outline the steps to build your cloud governance within your organisation.

• The first step is to identify the individuals who shall be included in the cloud governance program. The individuals should have a mixed skill set with an executive sponsor.

• Once the individuals have been identified and assigned roles, the scope of the program is set, the charter should be set to meet future needs, and the project scope should be defined.

• Come up with different project workstreams to assess the cloud and find out the different resources and security threats. The identified resources and vulnerabilities should be put in an inventory.

• Set the standards and policies for the monitoring and reporting must be immediate; the standards must be able to evolve with time to meet the comprehensive goals of compliance status across the organisation.

• The cycle of communication should be established at this stage which will be able to communicate when the programs us being formed.

• The coordination of deliverables with a deadline should be established for compliance.

• Resources should be allocated to make sure the project is successful.

- CHAPTER 11 -

Cloud Optimisation Strategy

Control & manage your organisation cloud costs

"Cloud computing is really a no-brainer for any start-up because it allows you to test your business plan very quickly for little money. Every start-up, or even a division within a company that has an idea for something new, should be figuring out how to use cloud computing in its plan."— Brad Jefferson

In recent years organisations have been moving workloads to the public cloud at an unprecedented rate, fuelled by unlimited scalability and lower IT costs, which only charge for resources used. The reality of the situation is you are charged for the cloud resources you ordered, whether they have been used. Cloud optimisation starts and stops with strategy, organisations give cloud optimisation little thought as the whole purpose of moving to the cloud is to save money, right?

Now that organisations are in the public cloud, they are faced with similar challenges of how to track and control public cloud spending. With a very agile team, there can be issues in managing resource deployment, oversizing of resources, shutting down of resources, but a mature cloud operating model should remediate these issues.

It is not in the financial interest of the public cloud provider to assist you in optimising your cloud spend. They do offer tools to monitor and predict usage but do not help find under-utilised or unused resources. Many fantastic third-party cloud optimisation solutions do a great job and are one of the quickest and cheapest ways to reduce cost.

The right cloud optimisation solution will help you identify opportunities for cost-saving and give recommendations on how to implement those savings, providing you with the ability and visibility to control your cloud spend. This approach is only one way of controlling costs and to stay on track, you need a long-term strategy to eliminate unnecessary cloud spend.

In this chapter, we shall discuss the options to manage and optimise your public cloud costs and workload performance.

PILLARS OF CLOUD OPTIMISATION

Cloud optimisation is about identifying the correct resources required for the workload to run and operate in the cloud efficiently. Each workload has its own unique resource requirements and will perform differently in the cloud over time. Often engineers deploy resources that are not required to facilitate a workload migration or overcome an application issue. There are eight cloud optimisation pillars that an organisation can use to optimise their cloud performance and costs.

1. Identify unused resources

It is so easy for engineers or developers to deploy VMs and resources in the public cloud to perform temporary tasks. We all have such a busy schedule, and it is easy to forget that these resources cost money and should be shut down when the task is completed. We have also come across engineers forgetting to remove storage after an instance has been retired. The two examples above happen quite often and result in additional spend for the organisation. A cloud optimisation strategy shall identify unused instanced, unattached storage and remove them from the environment.

2. Auto-Shutdown to reduce costs during off-hours

Once an instance is deployed, you are charged for every minute that workload is running in the cloud. The public cloud provider charges 730 hours per month, even if you do not use that resource. If that workload was not required at the weekend, you could auto-shutdown for 96 hours and save money as you are only charged when that resource is on.

3. Resizing for resources

Rightsizing identifies all the VMs in your environment that has incorrect resources allocated to run the workload. Resizing has the objective of minimising cost and maximise workload performance. The resizing cost optimisation does not stop with VMs and includes memory, databases, compute, storage and more. The right-sizing strategy is more than minimising cloud costs, and it maximises performance by resizing resources at peak time.

4. Reserved Instances

This is the easiest and quickest way to minimise cost in the public cloud is with RI. Your organisation commits to the public cloud for 1,2 or 3-year term.

Organisations committed to the cloud for the long-term should invest in RIs. These are large discounts based on upfront payment and time commitment. RI savings can reach up to 75%, so this is a must for cloud cost optimization. Since RIs can be purchased for one or three years, it is important to analyse your past usage and properly prepare for the future. To purchase RIs, see Microsoft's Azure Reserved VM Instances (RIs) purchasing guide or follow instructions in the AWS Management Console.

5. Consolidate Idle Resources

An idle instance may have a memory utilization level of 15%. However, organisations are billed for the entire cost of that instance, which is a waste. The cloud optimisation strategy would identify and consolidate into fewer instances.

6. Consider a single vendor

A multi-cloud approach is a valid strategy with many benefits, such as avoiding vendor lock-in. Organisations that implement a multi-vendor strategy risk losing out on volume discounts. The public cloud vendors all have different levels of volume discount subject to your yearly spend. Public cloud vendors reward organisations who have a significant spend via discounts. An organisation with spend across multiple cloud vendors may lose out on this volume discount due to not reaching the required cloud spend. There is also the hidden cost to a multi-cloud strategy such as administration tasks, traffic between platforms and training and hiring of staff across two different cloud platforms

7. Data and file management

The cloud vendors charge per TB for storage, to reduce this cost, you need to minimise your storage footprint. Compressing the data reduces your storage need and reduces your storage cost. Create rules to take advantage of the different storage types to delete data or move between data between the storage types. For Example, you may have active data on blob storage, but x percentage of this data is never accessed which should be moved to cold storage at a lower cheaper storage rate

8. Optimise architecture and service types \ model

The way your application is design can have a significant impact on your cloud costs. A typical application could use multiple VMs to run the workload, but could this application be implemented with PaaS or could containers be used to reduce costs? Strike a balance between cost and performance, finding the type of service and model that delivers the optimal cost savings and performance.

9. Use Serverless services

Serverless services remove the need for engineers to manage or configure cloud VMs. The engineer creates the code for the workload, and the serverless service manages the cloud infrastructure deployment, saving the engineers time on deploying the infrastructure.

Optimisation Case Studies – Real World

The case studies outlined below are of real-world organisations that I have helped to optimise their cloud costs using the different pillars of cloud optimisation.

Case Study #1

An organisation within the financial industry are operating their core applications in the Microsoft Azure platform. The initial cost of running the Azure service was grossly underestimated @ $32K per year, and the organisation was well over budget spending $110K per year. My team and I conducted an optimisation review and found that VMs where over spec, several VMs not been used, expensive storage was used where less expensive storage would be appropriate, and no reserved instance applied.

When my team applied the recommendations from the optimisation review, the organisation spend went for $110K to $43K per year, a saving of $67K.

Case Study #2

An organisation within the legal sector are operating their backup solution in the cloud. The organisation cloud storage cost is 75% over budget compared to what was estimated.

Once our team conducted an optimisation review, we found several issues like storage over-provisioning and incorrect use of the storage type.

When the storage was cleaned up, and the correct storage type applied, the organisation achieved a cost-saving from €75K to €24K per year, a cost-saving of €51K on storage alone.

CHALLENGES FACED BY ORGANISATIONS TO OPTIMISE THEIR PUBLIC CLOUD

From working with hundreds of organisations running a cloud environment, they all face very similar challenges when operating and managing costs in the cloud, like

Lack of visibility – The lack of visibility across an organisations cloud environment is a real challenge that needs to be resolved quickly. With no or very little visibility, the organisation cannot manage costs effectively, leading the organisation to be reactive instead of proactive. Many organisations have implemented a single pane of glass dashboard across the entire cloud environment to monitor and control cloud cost and performance metrics.

Ever-increasing cloud costs – cost keep increasing as your business grows and you receive unexpected high cloud bills.

Provisioning Management - Provisioning management is the management and allocation of cloud resources for workloads or projects. Poor Provisioning management leads to higher and unnecessary cloud costs, poor application performance and a poor experience for the users.

Governance – no governance controls in place to manage cloud purchasing, budgets and processes to switch off resources when they are not required,

Capacity planning – have no visibility to predict trends in infrastructure usage, so it's challenging to plan,

Migrations - unsure as to what it will cost to move workloads to the cloud.

Cloud billing complexity - The number of invoices, the complexity inside each invoice

STOP FLYING BLIND

To truly get control of your cloud spend, you need to understand at a deep level what resources you are using, who is using them, and when those resources are being used. Without the above information, you will never understand how your infrastructure works together and therefore cannot ensure you have the right capacity, at the right time or the right workloads turned off.

Organisations should fast-track the implementation of a cloud optimisation and cost control tool to help manage cloud costs. One of the objectives of a cloud optimisation tool is to give visibility to what you are spending.

Printed in Great Britain
by Amazon